The Strength

REVIEW COPY
Not For Resale

The Strength of Materials

Poems by Rhea Tregebov

Wolsak and Wynn . Toronto

© Rhea Tregebov 2001
All rights reserved. No part of this book may be reproduced or transmitted in any form, by any means, electronic or mechanical, without permission in writing from the publisher, except by a reviewer, who may quote brief passages in a review. In case of photocopying or other reprographic copying, a licence is required from CANCOPY (Canadian Copyright Licensing Agency), One Yonge Street, Suite 1900, Toronto, Ontario, Canada M5E 1E5.

Typeset in Garamond.
Printed in Canada by The Coach House Printing Company, Toronto.
Front cover art: "Rockport, New Brunswick" by Thaddeus Holownia
Cover design: The Coach House Printing Company, Toronto
Author's photograph: Peter Higdon

The author and the publisher gratefully acknowledge the Canada Council for the Arts and the Ontario Arts Council for their generous support. The author further acknowledges the support of the City of Toronto through the Toronto Arts Council.

The poems included in this book have been published in the following journals: *The Malahat Review*, *The New Quarterly*, *Arena* (Australia) and *La Traductière* (Paris). "Elegy for the Night" appeared under the title "The Room" in the anthology *A Room at the Heart of Things: The Work That Came to Me* (Véhicule Press, 1998), edited by Elisabeth Harvor. "Elegy for the Light," "A Really Good Run (Elegy)," "Elegy for the Given" and "Teacup Elegy," which appeared in *The Malahat Review*, received Honourable Mention in the poetry category for the 1998 National Magazine Awards.

Wolsak and Wynn Publishers Ltd, 192 Spadina Avenue, Suite 315, Toronto, Ontario, Canada M5T 2C2

National Library of Canada Cataloguing in Publication Data
Tregebov, Rhea, 1953-
    The Strength of Materials
Poems.
ISBN 0-919897-76-2
I. Title
PS8589.R342S77 2001   C811'.54   C2001-930591-5
PR9199.3.T73S77 2001

*for my father, Sam Block
whose strength I'm learning
whose tenderness I've always known*

Words lead to deeds. They prepare the soul, make it ready, and move it to tenderness.

—Saint Teresa

Rousseau (in his *Discourse on the Origin of Inequality* and his *Essay on the Origin of Language*) conceives of a primordial or original human language, in which everything has its true and natural name; a language so concrete, so particular, that it can catch the essence, the "itness", of everything; so spontaneous that it expresses all emotion directly; and so transparent that it is incapable of any evasion or deception. Such a language would be without (and indeed would have no need for) logic, grammar, metaphor, or abstractions—it would be language not mediate, a symbolic expression of thought and feelings, but, almost magically, an *im*mediate one. Perhaps the thought of such a language—a language of the heart, a language of perfect transparency and lucidity, a language that can say everything, without ever deceiving or entangling us (Wittgenstein spoke of the bewitchment of language), a language as pure and profound as music—is a universal fantasy.

—Oliver Sacks, *Seeing Voices*

CONTENTS

Subway Elegy 11
Elegy for the Light 12
Intelligent Life: Elegy 14
Elegy for the World 15
The Black Mitt (Elegy) 16

Elegy for Knowing 19

Elegy for the Dawn 29
Light Elegy 30
Elegy for the Dead 31
Elegy for the Wolf 32
List (Elegy) 33

Into the World (Elegy) 37

Elegy for the Self (Vermeer's "Lacemaker") 47
A Really Good Run (Elegy) 48
Elegy for the Garden 49
Elegy for the Wild 50
Train Elegy 51
Elegy for the Sky 52
Elegy for the Afternoon 53
Two Weeks (Elegy) 54
Heartbreak Hill (Elegy for the Marathon) 55
Hell's Kitchen (Elegy) 56
Elegy for the Night 57
Elegy for Elegies 59
Elegy for the Day 61
Spring (Elegy) 62

June Elegy   63
Gift (Elegy)   64
Elegy for the Given   65
Elegy for the Gift (Elegy for the Light)   66
Paris Elegy (Atget)   67
Waste (Elegy)   68
Elegy for Want   71
Teacup Elegy   72
Elegy for the Sparrow   73

Notes   75

Subway Elegy

Sometimes what I want
is for you to lay your body on mine
so that I know my own extent,
know where to stop. Me,
not me. Who do I love and
where do I stop loving?
Nothing in my body mourns
the death of a star in Ursa Major.
But the woman in Sarajevo
her boy's ten-year-old life
leaking through her hands
staining the cheap sweater
she could have bought up the street
at Zeller's, the boy's Adidas sneakers
unlaced by the blast—
to her my body replies,
mouth drawn inward, teeth
pulling at my bottom lip
and I go for my own boy's unscathed
head, pull his body back to me.
My sensible boy, who has seen
all kinds of TV death unmoved,
the boy who looks up at me,
his breath indrawn, hand to my shoulder,
when three die in the subway crash
at our local stop:
It could have been me.

Elegy for the Light
Forty-third parallel, December

All this December as the light diminishes
we eat sweet small oranges from Spain,
their quick-zip peels spraying tart
on our fingers, small suns we eat.

I get on the bus in daylight, abstracted;
spend some minutes absorbing the faces
of fellow travellers, and when I look up,
look up to a darkness come so fast—
as though these faces had drunk the light.
And I'm afraid my face also has gone dark,
extinguished.

The streetlights are on,
and I want to remember that the light will come back,
that it's because of the angle of the earth's rotation,
because we're in the temperate zone
that we have seasons,
that things change and change and change.
But this year even change has been disorderly.
Today in December the air bewilderingly mild;
my star-of-Bethlehem poking dumb
green spikes out of winter dirt
below the honey-locust tree just in time
for Christmas or a killing frost.

Smell of orange on my fingers,
I step onto the rubber matting.
The door opens.
I don't believe in resurrection.
I have one life: what
if it fills with darkness?

INTELLIGENT LIFE: ELEGY

Home from a long trip I find
the familiar rooms grown wider, and
me suddenly small, on the broad streets
of childhood. Small, like that, and
lonely. It's lonely here.
We think that down here,
on the planet, there's abundance; that
it's out there that warmth is an aberration—
the scientist sending out messages
looking for intelligent life, thinking
he may have located a likely solar system.
I don't know.
Take my friend from the former Yugoslavia
sitting inland, strong fingers splayed
on her knees, cold, remembering the sea.
Or my aunt, also inland, adrift, her memory
riffling like ripe wind through a wheat field—
she wakes, cold and afraid, to bury the husband
dead three years now. It's lonely here.
Take me. I have only my own body.
I nod to the neighbour,
leave messages for my best friend,
eat dinner with the radio on.
Don't tell me about lovers
on the shadowy grass, foreheads close,
whispering a world. The delicate
joints of equipment adjust, slo-mo,
bend like sunflowers to catch a reply.
Me, I'm looking too.

Elegy for the World

Late January; a long cold. The snow
is tired of the world. It wants
to set the world at rest, to settle
accounts: fence rail, flax stalk,
ash. It will ease this world
out of itself, make a new,
white, order. Will hush
each boot print, fall
and fill each emptiness,
hollow; fall and not
cease.

The Black Mitt (Elegy)

The black mitt curled, coiled, dirty against the dirty snow,
its thumb chewed to a ragged stump. The pair of brown loafers
resting, on the lowest, broken, branch of a balsam shrub,
in an aspect of expectation, the left one slightly askew,
as though their owner had lifted off, and they were the last traces
of some secular Assumption. What wanders the world:
keys, scarves, umbrellas; hair clips, hubcaps, bicycle locks.
The belt loose in the gutter, the dog's leash without dog,
without owner. Things get away
                                                though others collect
in the backs of closets, on windowsills; in empty yogurt
containers, biscuit tins: ticket stubs from baseball games,
empty spools for thread, the wooden ones; plastic balls
the colour of candy that you almost want to bite into;
a Pez container with a Goofy head, its rectangular candies
long gone or gone stale; screws belonging to what?; inscrutable
trapezoidal nuggets of black plastic; the mateless sock, mitt. Us.

Elegy for Knowing

1.

Name the countries that border Rumania.
I don't know.

2.

Moon in the branches.
A few leaves huddle in clumps,
shivering like sparrows.
The ones that have fallen pile themselves
in the precise pattern the wind wants.
What do I know? It's easy to believe
in constancy, to believe the moon,
say, despite its changes, has
always been there. It hasn't.

3.

What you don't know can't hurt you
is a lie. I've always been afraid
of knowing, not knowing. Think
of my grandfather, father, uncles
at the Seder table, waiting for the bad
word, the syllable gone wrong,
to raise their chorus of correction,
keep us from damaging God.

4.

But to move from not knowing to knowing—
there's a dangerous space. Where do you go
in between the not and the knowing, what
becomes of you?

5.

The gloss, boss of that instrument, dusted,
polished for thirty years and not much used.
Twenty years past lessons, stiff,
my fingers pick out notes on my mother's piano,
and they come into melody. Downstairs,
in the orderly basement, opening the rounded,
studded lid of a trunk, I find books,
and from the books, Hebrew characters
and they come into sound on my lips, come into words.

6.

Name the countries that border Rumania. No.
I didn't want to know, wanted
to believe only what the body believed,
to feel the sidewalk sun-hot
through my thongs, on my skinny shoulders,
to lick a lime-green Popsicle, and be
in my body, the body happy
and me, in it, happy of it.

7.

What I didn't let myself know
hurt me. What does my body
remember? My mouth knowing yours,
your body in me.

ELEGY FOR THE DAWN

"Abandonado como las muelles en el alba."
[Deserted like the wharves at dawn.]

So much stillness. The docks
breathe, set sailors asleep
in the moon's steep pull.
There, at the blue edge,
the sky seems to touch the sea.
It doesn't. The wharves
waiting, alone.

Light Elegy

"*Y la ternura, leve como el agua y la harina*"
[And tenderness, light as water, dust]

and the fool, who wants
to hold, remember, everything:
you touch me, tips
of your fingers tender my neck, diagram
the knots of spine, flesh of shoulder.
There. You drew me
to you; your body let me in.
Not you. I want to remember
everything because it's gone.

Elegy for the Dead

"*Y la palabra apenas comenzada en los labios.*"
[And the word scarce begun on the lips.]

She wants the dead to help her.
The dead who got there, lived their lives to the end.
She looks at her hands. Where did they get her,
what will she do with her hands.
How does she walk the earth in a body, still of
this world, in it, though she wants none of it.
How is it the heart continues, with so much
happiness useless, because it didn't make a life.
The dead. What do the dead know. Though
she looks at their gone faces, though
they come back in dreams, in passing strangers,
they tell us nothing now. What help are they.

Elegy for the Wolf

"*Y la ternura...*"
[And tenderness...]

If it's true, next life
you'll come back a wolf
have only hunger and
the wish for a mouth
full of blood and meat
you'll come a wolf
in December
the long hard run
and nothing

List (Elegy)

"*...leve como el agua y la harina*"
[...light as water, dust]

Thin milk poured
into the glass:
starved, starved, it says;
then it's gone. So
you write up a list:
milk & eggs. Think
milk & eggs. This
is what you have to do
and not think *sorrow*,
not think *but, but*.
Only. Milk & eggs.
This is what you have to do.

Into the World (Elegy)

"Nature has no outline, but Imagination has."

—William Blake, *Notebooks*

1.

I'm sober, and everyone else is drunk.
I'm always sober. Upright
on my barstool, people around me spilling,
buddy, into each others' pockets, raucous
breath in beery faces
and I'm outlined in black crayon,
I have edges.

2.

I have edges, but they bend.
One day I'm walking up an ordinary street
and everywhere I look women are waistless,
led by our bellies. We're walking
up the ordinary streets and don't know
what we're getting ourselves into,
don't know that our lives will no longer
be our own, they'll be
everyone else's.

3.

It's work bringing my boy into the world.
He's distracted, head cocked,
tuned to some tangential thought,
askance to what he really should
be thinking about, a primary
idea: being born. *Push*, they say.
I can't not. We're both
taken, part of something else.
Then, pushed, that first yelp
of air, joy, or terror, breathing
all on his lonesome. And he's
one person. And so am I.

4.

Other women speak of the alien
moment their good bodies went awry.
But for me, it was the usual,
a body I'd never believed in
having its way.

5.

I didn't ask to be born.
He's bent out of shape, the boy,
angry that he's not grown up, that he's got
a mother. So skinny sideways, he's a stick
of chewing gum wrapped in foil, can flex.
And he wants to test himself, press
against the edges; does chin-ups, curls.
Pushes against the hard air, against
the world and what it will and won't let him have,
until he's changed, shaped a new boy.

6.

Some mornings I turn my face to the window,
its sun, or cloud, and then turn away:
I didn't ask to be born.
To be shoved out into this,
where I am one person. *Push.*
I want to be saved from life. To be
still, under the ground, live
with stones and the hungry
roots of trees.

7.

Those mornings, even babies make me sad:
the way they love the world, the way
they let it filter through them.
Because I'm afraid they'll be spoiled,
go brown at their edges, like fruit;
that their lives will sour, curdle.
But by noon, the boy bangs into the room,
hungry, to bend the emptiness and, *buddy*,
the lush green world insists, *ah friend*,
this is no way to feel; turn to the window,
the lovely world, take all it wants.

ELEGY FOR THE SELF (VERMEER'S "LACEMAKER")

She is nowhere:
no background to her foreground
just the grey plane of what may
be a wall, may be nothingness,
her life.

She's not painted;
there is no painter. She's not
thinking, not being watched.
She's making a living;

she's working.
Quiet and self and labour;
she furnishes
the sacred real.

A Really Good Run (Elegy)

I finish my run and think
I'm so strong now, nothing could kill me:
not the dwarf star imploding in Alpha Centauri, not
the Toronto Humane Society van swerving to avoid a racoon.
Not living beside Lake Ontario, not Devon cream or rare
roast beef, chlorinated, fluoridated water. Not booze,
drugs, sex, black ice on the sidewalk. Not seeing my aunt
go down my front steps, whispering, *It hurts so much.*
Or my strong father stalled by his hip after half
a block, leaning against a telephone pole.

ELEGY FOR THE GARDEN

What's she doing in the garden?
The boy wants his mother
to stop whatever it is and mind
him. It's the first warm day,
the very first, and she's hauling
a winter of rubbish. The fall was awful,
everything neglected, the winter
worse but now things want doing.
The green things want her. The garden steep,
in the mouth of the traffic;
everything growing there strong.
The boy gives up, heads over to a friend's.
She's too dirty to hug. One foot set on a rock,
the other on a bare bit of soil, she's more woman
than mother, more goat than woman.
She's almost parallel the incline,
tearing at what's dead, remembering
at last what she planted, what she loves.

Elegy for the Wild

Trees and sky, the woman behind me says, *just trees and sky*.
On the bus north to Sudbury the land fills me up.
I think we think we're more important than we are.
Three rows back a kid coos
like a pigeon, ready for sleep,
a dream of trees.
Beautiful wild country.
Now the boy's a soft, mournful siren.
He's tired, he's so tired and the bus
is a rough cradle. It's May,
and snow still stands in the deepest shade,
in the place where it's always winter.
I want to keep looking.
I want to keep looking till I'm done.
Country. Beautiful country. Beautiful wild country.

Train Elegy

Llamas sporting in the Ontario fields.
A new porch on an old house.
Everything slips by the train's windows.
Trillium, mouths open, eyes bright.
Faint green fizz of leaves on the birches.
Stumps in the unploughed earth, rocks white
as the shoulders of the dead, surfacing.
Water in ditches running thinly
almost as fast as the train, spring
run-off flooding the fields, making
the rivers high and wild.
On the imperfect rails the car
is a fluid, sloshing side to side
over its centre of gravity, lullaby.
Sh. See everything,
but don't touch.
As soon as you have it, you
lose it, loose it into the world.

Elegy for the Sky

Thunder takes us up, against our bodies'
best knowledge, against all certainty,
into the impossible stuff of clouds.
So much we can do, do do because we can.
Without thinking, though, without
imagining consequences and so
we tear the sky with every flight,
let in the ordinary harm it once kept us from.

Elegy for the Afternoon

Don't gawk,
the woman with the broom said.
Or didn't say, but I saw her face
as she went to her sweeping
as if that was the right thing to do.
It ate up the afternoon.
I've never seen blood like that—
a neat trail downhill, steady,
like it meant business.
The crunch I thought was metal on metal.
The woman with the broom
bringing a mug of water to the driver
who sat there drinking, shaking,
then set the mug on the curb.
The old guy curled around himself
on the pavement like that was his special place.
Sirens, cops, ambulance guys; they did CPR
and then they stopped. Even so
they were busy with it: yellow tape, cameras,
numbers called out across the hot concrete.
Finally they hosed down the pavement.
Someone must've been waiting,
fiddling with a purse or flicking channels.
I keep thinking of the shoe,
the one that landed on the woman's steps.
Stop sweeping, the cop said, *leave the shoe where it is.*

Two Weeks (Elegy)

Your children are with you for two
whole weeks and your heart,
which has been dislocated
somewhere between where they are
and where they should be,
goes back into your body. You need
nothing now, nothing but their voices
in the next room, the youngest
singing along with the dinosaur,
the older one chiding, needling.
You need nothing more.

Heartbreak Hill (Elegy for the Marathon)

Don't even start if you're not going to finish.
No half-hearted tries, no half measures here,
though you wonder why you want to get there;
go through all that ache for what.
Heart banging against your ribs,
surge of blood in the ears and all
the small muscles in your knees a hapless choir.
You're too old for this; anyone is.
There were options: go around,
stop short, never have begun. But you want
to look back at what you did, at a life that was
too soft, too many easy choices; fear. You want
to finish; want that whiff of catalpa,
something both outside and in you.

HELL'S KITCHEN (ELEGY)

Yellow gingham curtains,
a countertop washed
and washed clean.
It bears the weight
of her hands as they listen
for the car door, the click
of the key, beloved,
in the latch.

ELEGY FOR THE NIGHT

When it's bad, the plastic of the oxygen tent,
wavering intervention, comes between her and the room,
the square edges warble against her sight.
Back behind her head, to the left, where the corridor is,
the nursing station where help might come. In the daytime
carts roll down the corridor, chatter of china
on steel, silver covers on white plates of food
she can't eat. Where is the clock? Hitchcock clock
she can't see but feels, she can feel the hands move
and not move, move slow against the heaviness
                              of the room. She can't go
into the corridor, she can turn her head but she can't get up,
she can't get out of the bed, she wants her mother.
It's 3:15, 3:17, 3:21 she's waiting for four o'clock.
It's 4:02 her mother isn't here but suddenly
she stands at the foot of the bed it's all right
but the doctors say four to six. At six
her mother goes, takes her hands, takes her
voice away with her. The room goes grey
and the corridor that must be there is quiet
except for the nurses' voices.
Once, twice, they check in, good girl,
hand on her forehead. With the darkness
it comes down on her chest but if she's very still
it gets pushed to the edges. Breathe quiet now,

don't let it get you. Breathe quiet and believe
time is not still. Shadows slide along the bar of light
in the doorway. They're not alive. Something
makes those shadows the way something makes
the shadows that arc along the walls, the ceiling
of her room at home. Cars, their headlights.
The shadows go on and night doesn't end
and she learns you have to do what you can't do.
The nurses' voices begin to drift and she's
sliding down and then it's morning.

ELEGY FOR ELEGIES

1.

I have no place to go but up, no way
to squeeze back down past faces and arms.
Goosebumps prickling my skin,
the elbows of older, taller children;
clammy grip of wet bathing suits.
My chin at someone's heels, someone else's chin
at my heels, we are a ladder of determination, up
and up to the five-metre platform.
My turn. Someone waits as I bring my arms back,
then swing them high, knees bent. Soft breath
behind me, as my toes tense at the edge,
knees, calves, thighs locked. Someone waits
but further down the line someone whispers,
jeers. I'm the girl who has decided to jump
but there's another I who will not proceed
and I stall in her body, its own decision,
until shame or stubbornness drives me forward at last
and down into a blue that receives but doesn't end me.

2.

A chute of intention has carried me here,
to the reconstructed cattlecar
in Washington's Holocaust Museum.
Carried me through each tactful exhibit
so that I can see enough but not so much
that I stop seeing; has got me here
to the doorway but the dark interior, no.
No. In its wisdom, the body refuses
and I stall again until stubbornness or shame
drives me forward at last and it is as if
I were down into a dark that receives me,
my shoulder at someone's back, someone else's
shoulder at my back. Someone waits at my back, from
someone further down the line a crushed whisper.
We are a parcel of intention, but not our own.

ELEGY FOR THE DAY

The weather teases out the last days of May,
cool wind easing the first blooms of iris, late tulips:
a white-gloved traffic cop serenely holding one season back
so the other can clear the intersection. Wait. Wait for me.
Let's not rush into this summer thing. I want to dig in my heels,
I want May, the shiny light of new leaves. Want to be in
my body, taste food, sleep the sleep of the just.
We work too hard in this city, running on empty, and days
go. I want them back, want to break bread—no—
the filmy crisp layers of croissant, spread with raspberry
jam and crème fraîche, want the morning to doze
slowly by, the daily scattered over the bed; to yawn
in my kimono and reach for another kiss, sun heavy
on the bedclothes, sounds drifting in from the street
below in another language, those idle passersby who
don't know how happy we are upstairs, lazed, easy, in our bed.

Spring (Elegy)

I sit in the spring
sunlight and inhabit my body,
watch ferns unfold.
There are too many
red tulips, but I abide.
I suffer the sun
to sit on me.
I don't think, or think
differently. An ant
interests me.
The stiff shift
of the tulip in wind
interests me.
The tulips open,
cups for the sun.
I trust the sun,
the shadow, that make
a gothic arch
where the petals overlap.
Then the real
cat scratches at
the screen. He wants
out.

June Elegy
Major Street, Toronto

The yard that has room in its heart for
one rosebush.
The yard with slim yellow irises.
The yard with gravel.
The yard with the wrought-iron fence,
box hedge; the gate snapping shut
like a change purse. The yard pursed.
The yard with roses that have no thorns, none,
the smell of raspberry jam.
The yard with columbine and columbine and columbine.
The yard with thistle and crabgrass spiking two feet into the air.
The one wistful with wisteria, drooping.
The one with forget-me-nots in a filmy ring, trimmed lilac,
tea roses handcuffed to a stake, about to bloom.
The yard with garbage cans.
The yard with tricycles.
With sunlight.
Trash.
The yard with snow-in-summer, honey locust,
star-of-Bethlehem, periwinkle,
in bloom.

Gift (Elegy)

I'm trying to sleep,
to make my thoughts sheets
on the clothes-tree
in my mother's yard, white
against the blue sky, sharp
as risen loaves, then dull,
lank on the lines. Sheets
that semaphore *here,*
here, listen to me, but
I want my mind blank, full
as loaves about to bake, open
as sheets to sleep.

ELEGY FOR THE GIVEN

That on the southbound Bathurst bus
the voice at my elbow is speaking Russian,
the one at my back Portuguese perhaps, or Spanish.
That the air is grey and smells, as I walk down Bathurst,
successively, of exhaust, burnt toast, ozone,
alyssum. That on the northeast corner
of Bathurst and Bloor a man lies asleep or
unconscious or dead in his vomit and I walk by.
That on the southeast corner a middle-aged man
in shirtsleeves sells his god in a magazine
called *Awake* and all of us walk by.
That the young man going east on rollerblades
amid the cursing drivers has a ring through his eyebrow
and a peace symbol on his black leather jacket.
That at the Shoppers' Drug Mart three blocks east
I can choose from 62 kinds of toothpaste.
That rose of Sharon blooms
mauve to the south and white to the north
of the entry to the Aston Court. That
summer is come whether I want it or not.

ELEGY FOR THE GIFT (ELEGY FOR THE LIGHT)

Sometimes, when the subway car
comes briefly out of the tunnel,
we don't look up, miss the light.
And it's as though, inattentive,
we'd never had that moment
of brightness. A life might be full
of such small losses or full,
equally, of small, dense gifts:
the child on that same car
dipping her face into her mother's,
that perfect regard.

Paris Elegy (Atget)

"How private and public spheres intersect" and
how it is observed, tacitly, that trees,
in twenty-five years, grow but buildings
do not; how light, how stillness, how
back lanes, courtyards, jumble and give
civil cohesion; how light bleeding in the gap
between buildings on the narrow street
dissolves the boundaries of walls, opens;
how people blur, are fugitive, illusive,
dark, concealed, afraid of what he will show
them, show of them; how the stones, edifices,
pavement emerge, in his lens, become beloved,
human.

WASTE (ELEGY)

1.

Look out the window: the trees
waste the sky, the wind wastes itself
across the indifferent faces of buildings.
Ah, but we love it, waste; let
the sun waste itself on concrete,
words waste themselves on the page.
What have we done with this love?
What have we done now? *It's too much*,
we say, *too much*. We have
a crisis of too much.

2.

But not everywhere. We've seen
the pixel images—the seagulls,
flocks of human families lighting
on Himalayas of waste, making a life
of what someone else, us, didn't
want: didn't want to eat, wear,
carry, bear, any more. They cry
and cry, thin calls stitching the sky
above the gay, coat-of-many-colours stink.

3.

We have a crisis of too much; plan
railcars, trucks, barges to carry it away.
Why not have them here, beside us?
Have them walk with us as we crumple
the box from donuts, cram it in the bin;
let their hands save us. Bring them here
and the world will settle into balance;
have them with us, safe,
the world one just place.

ELEGY FOR WANT

I would wish you a clean life with numbers,
their sureness, their cool and stable surfaces—
a leather bomber jacket polishing your broad young
shoulders, the spell of faculty across your back—
but it's words you want, isn't it?
I can tell by the way you take up books,
by your face when you listen: it's words
you're hungry for, their taste, the way
syllables work your tongue. And you won't
hold them cold or bloodless in an educated mouth,
they won't slip against each other, tight and sleek;
you'll have friction, you'll have them salt and wet.
I wish you what you want.

Teacup Elegy

Sunlight and I've got this cup
of coffee. Teacup, coffee cup.
Cup of light. What are we the containers of, what
do we hold? Take lambs, limbs
new to the earth. Something enters the cell,
cluster of being, some frolic in the cell
brings them to earth, brings them up
from knees to hooves. Cup warm
against my palm like the ewe's flank against
the lamb's muzzle. My son's newborn face a not-yet-human
face, the blind, kittenish mind feeling its way
home. We are become different from the lamb,
the lamb different from the stones its skittery hooves stumble on.
Pocketing the rock I picked from the cold Atlantic,
I thumbed its surface till it held my hand's warmth,
pressed my face against the rock face I was climbing.
Carbon, silicon, hydrogen—the rock and I are organized
in a different geometry and different. Sunlight
kicks us into being, licks windowsill, teacup, me.

ELEGY FOR THE SPARROW

What's the point, the sullen boy asks,
of learning their names? *Bird*
should do. The indistinct grey of wings
against concrete, droppings on the faded fence.
And in spring, a racket at dawn, nuisance
of yellow gum, smashed eggshell, white
or blue, on the hard-hearted pavement. And he's sullen
for a reason. The city hard this winter,
with its tests and arguments; its losses.
His mother in one house, father in another.
And now it's spring. So what. Birds,
and their names, and the guide
so sure it's important. Like an ache,
this arch of branch over his head, glint
of light on the water. Something moves
in the space between words. Streak of smeared white
on his left and a call. Gull.
He knows that one.
Dun, dumb gull, gullible;
gull diving for nothing, for his fake toss
off the ferry. The island phoney too,
little stretch of green at the city's edge,
its quiet, the lift of the leaves
against the wind. But the city's still there,
ten minutes across the harbour.
And this blue—but the water's trash too:
pop cans and plastic bags, gasoline slicks,
little spills like the eyes in peacock feathers.
Peacock names itself, but the others?

As if you could know them
by their names: house from song
sparrow, the black or the greyish streaks,
reddish tail or chestnut bar through the eyes.
Know them with your eyes closed:
three sweet notes, then a lower note, then
a trill; or chirp, cheep, and various twitters.
Song. House. Do they belong to him now, the way he
belongs to his mother, father, the way his parents belong
to him? As if words belonged to the things they name.
Things named for colour, the lilac lilac,
orange orange. What will the world give him
if he knows its names? House. Song. The word *snake*
leaping to his mouth at the striped ribbon at his feet,
its green slip through the grass.

NOTES

Thanks to Erin Mouré's "Ocean Poem" (*Furious*, House of Anansi, 1988) for the locution of the second line in "Elegy for Knowing" (3).

The epigrams in Spanish in "Elegy for the Dawn," "Light Elegy," "Elegy for the Dead," "Elegy for the Wolf" and "List (Elegy)" are from Pablo Neruda's poem, *La Canción Desesperada* [The Song of Despair] in *Veinte Poemas de Amor y Una Canción Desesperada* [Twenty Love Poems and a Song of Despair]. Translation the author's.

The phrase in quotations in "Paris Elegy (Atget)" is from the catalogue for the exhibit "Paris Itineraries: Photographs by Eugène Atget," shown at the Art Gallery of Ontario in March, 2001.

OTHER BOOKS OF POETRY BY RHEA TREGEBOV

Mapping the Chaos. Véhicule Press/Signal Editions, 1995 (1998).

The Proving Grounds. Véhicule Press/Signal Editions, 1991.

No One We Know. Mercury/Aya Press, 1986.

Remembering History. Guernica Editions, 1982.